Classical Guitar Method
Volume Two

By Bradford Werner
wernerguitareditions.com
thisisclassicalguitar.com
2017 Edition

Classical Guitar Method - Volume Two

by Bradford Werner
2017 Edition

Distributed by
wernerguitareditions.com
thisisclassicalguitar.com

© Bradford C. Werner 2017
All Rights Reserved.

Printing the PDF
This PDF has been designed for double sided printing. Place it in a three ring binder with dividers for each section. Binders are great as you can easily supplement it with extra materials of interest to the student and/or teacher. You are *not* permitted to print and *sell* this book.

Hard Copies
Print editions of this book are available at: thisisclassicalguitar.com or wernerguitareditions.com

Special Thanks
Uroš Barič, Michael Dias, Erin Fisher, Natasha Pashchenko, and Adrian Verdejo.

Classical Guitar Method
Volume Two

By Bradford Werner
wernerguitareditions.com
thisisclassicalguitar.com
2017 Edition

Classical Guitar Method - Volume Two

by Bradford Werner
2017 Edition

Distributed by
wernerguitareditions.com
thisisclassicalguitar.com

© Bradford C. Werner 2017
All Rights Reserved.

Printing the PDF
This PDF has been designed for double sided printing. Place it in a three ring binder with dividers for each section. Binders are great as you can easily supplement it with extra materials of interest to the student and/or teacher. You are *not* permitted to print and *sell* this book.

Hard Copies
Print editions of this book are available at: thisisclassicalguitar.com or wernerguitareditions.com

Special Thanks
Uroš Barič, Michael Dias, Erin Fisher, Natasha Pashchenko, and Adrian Verdejo.

Contents

Preface
- 6   Scales & Key Signatures
- 9   Chords & Chord Progressions
- 10   Introduction to Barres, Slurs & Position Playing

Part 1 - Reading Music & Chords in Common Keys
- 13   C Major - Menuet by Rameau (Duet), Allegro by Carulli, Morning Has Broken
- 17   A Minor - Romance by Küffner (Duet), Prelude by Carcassi, Star of County Down
- 21   G Major - Andante by Carulli (Duet), Simple Gifts (Arranging)
- 24   E Minor - Erster Verlust by Schumann (Duet), Prelude by Carcassi
- 27   D Major - La Petit Rien by Couperin (Duet), Rujero by Sanz
- 30   A Major - Menuet by Handel (Duet), Prelude by Carulli, Bound for South Australia
- 34   E Major - Gavotte by Corelli (Duet), Study No. 15 Op.60 by Sor
- 37   F Major - Prelude by Walther (Duet), Tempo di Marcia by Mertz
- 40   D Minor - Riguadon by Rameau (Duet), Folies d'Espagne
- 43   Bb Major - Bourrée by Telemann (Duet)

Part 2 - Introduction to 3rd & 5th Position
- 45   Single String Chromatic Scales
- 46   Introduction to 3rd & 5th Position with TAB
- 47   Introduction to 3rd & 5th Position, Ode to Joy, Exercises No. 1-10
- 51   Joy to the World, Minuet by Roncalli (Duet), El Not de la Mare (Duet), Estudio by Tarrega
- 55   Position Shifts, Canaries or the Hay (Duet), Feng Yang Flower Drum, Captain O'Kane

Part 3 - Rhythm Training
- 59   Tips for Counting Rhythms
- 61   Familiar Rhythmic Groupings
- 63   Time Signature & Rhythm Exercises on Open Strings No.1-60

Part 4 - Technique & Warm-up Exercises
- 76   Right Hand Exercises (walking, arpeggios, speed and stability)
- 84   Left Hand & Synchronization Exercises (placement, independence, slurs, scales)

About this book

This book teaches classical and fingerstyle guitar skills with a focus on reading tonal music. It includes solos, duos, chords, and exercises, giving students a well-rounded and enjoyable musical experience. Designed as a manageable amount of material, it supplements weekly lessons and prepares students for early intermediate repertoire. The four sections of study allow students to focus on specific strengths and weaknesses in the learning process.

Playing Level & Expectations

The goal of this book is to prepare students for repertoire at approximately RCM Toronto grade one level. Some of the solo pieces exceed this level offering ambitious students appropriate challenges. Because repertoire at this level rarely explores upper positions or difficult key signatures, the material has been limited to common keys and 3rd and 5th position playing. Further skills and knowledge are explored in the Volume 3 method book.

How to use this book

- Study all four parts of this book simultaneously. Attention to Part 4 (rhythm training) will prepare students for the variety of rhythms encountered in solos and duets.
- Use this book for the first half of weekly lessons with a qualified teacher. The second half of lessons should be dedicated to concert repertoire, theory, and special interests.
- Watch the video lessons to gain context as well as musical and technical advice. I have limited the textual information in this book in favour of providing free video lessons.

Free video lessons for this method

Video lessons on musicality and technique are available to supplement the material in this book. Find the list of lessons on the sales page for this book at thisisclassicalguitar.com or wernerguitareditions.com

Use of the 4th finger on upper strings

Students are often confused by inconsistencies in the fingering of scales vs repertoire. The intention of this book is to develop a balanced and adaptable left hand that is prepared for repertoire. The use of the 4th finger on D and G on the top two strings is required during repertoire and is, therefore, emphasized throughout this book. It is acceptable to use the 3rd finger when playing scales, exercises, or observing a one-finger-per-fret rule but students who are prone to avoiding the 4th finger during repertoire should consistently use it until the habit is firmly established. Trust the advice of your teacher if they re-finger anything.

Method Book Volume 3

Volume 3 focuses on solo repertoire lessons, expanded chord knowledge, and sight reading in upper positions. The main goal is to transition students firmly into the intermediate level of approximately RCM Toronto grade three or four.

Playing with fingernails in the right hand

Growing and shaping fingernails offers more control over technique and tone production but don't rush into it. If you feel overwhelmed by reading and playing, continue without nails while focusing on posture, hand positions, and reading. Once you feel comfortable with the playing level, see the lesson on nails: thisisclassicalguitar.com/fingernails-on-classical-guitar/

Recommended books to use <u>with</u> this method

- RCM Preparatory & Grade One Repertoire & Etudes - Historical and contemporary compositions from the Royal Conservatory of Music Toronto: amzn.to/2vgTA6F
- Celebrate Theory (Grade One & Two) - Theory from the RCM Toronto: amzn.to/2qgpHyJ
- Ricardo Iznaola on Practicing – Practice well, habits & philosophy: http://amzn.to/2hGBcdE

Recommended books to use <u>after</u> this method

- Classical Guitar Method Volume 3 (wernerguitareditions.com)
- Classical Guitar Technique Exercises (wernerguitareditions.com)
- Sight Reading for Classical Guitar Level IV-V by Robert Benedict: http://amzn.to/2g7NM53

Recommended gear for this level

- Seiko Quartz Metronome - Easy to use and a nice sound: http://amzn.to/2kbzCpz
- D'Addario NS Micro Clip-On Tuner - Low profile, works great: http://amzn.to/2pecdpN
- Zoom H1 – Audio Recorder - Record yourself as a practice tool: http://amzn.to/2hGKlmC

Follow the website for free lessons, sheet music, and pro videos

- Free and premium sheet music & tab: wernerguitareditions.com
- Free video lessons and instructional articles: thisisclassicalguitar.com/lessons/
- Gear, Strings, & Reviews: thisisclassicalguitar.com/classical-guitar-store-reviews/
- Email Newsletter: I send out an email newsletter filled with lessons, sheet music, pro videos and more. You can sign up at the website or here: eepurl.com/hGOak

Major Scale Theory

Two types of **intervals** must be understood before learning how major scales are constructed.
A **Half Step** is the distance from one pitch to another or one fret to the next on the guitar.
A **Whole Step** is the distance of two pitches or two frets on the guitar.

The pattern of whole and half steps that create major scales are:
whole - whole - half - whole - whole - whole - half

C Major

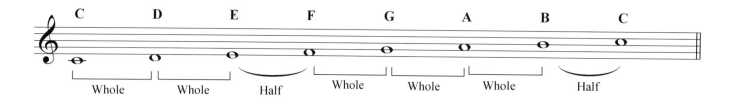

G Major

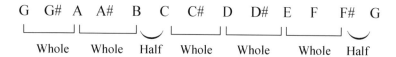

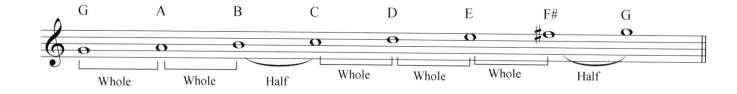

G Major with Key Signature

Key signatures are placed at the beginning of the staff and state which notes are sharp or flat within a key. Therefore, there is no need to write accidentals next to each note. This key signature states that all the F's are played as F#'s unless otherwise indicated.

© Bradford Werner 2017, Victoria, BC, Canada
Free & Premium Sheet Music & Tab: wernerguitareditions.com
Lessons, Pro Video, & Blog: thisisclassicalguitar.com

F Major with Key Signature
Bb is used instead of A# because we always proceed to a new note on the staff and avoid accidentals.

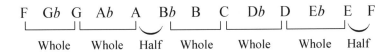

Key Signatures
Memorize the number of sharps or flats in each key up to four sharps and flats.

Moving through sharp keys in 5ths
Notice how the keys using sharps move up in 5ths
You can count up five to the next key, for example: **C**, D, E, F **G** and then **G**, A, B, C, **D**
Also notice that the sharps in the key signature move in fifths (F# - C# and then C# - G#).

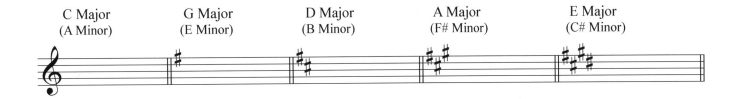

Moving through flat keys in 4ths
Notice how the keys using flats move up in 4ths.

© Bradford Werner 2017, Victoria, BC, Canada
Free & Premium Sheet Music & Tab: wernerguitareditions.com
Lessons, Pro Video, & Blog: thisisclassicalguitar.com

Relative Minor Keys

Every major key has a relative minor key that shares the same key signature.
Minor scales are formed by starting on the 6th scale degree of their relative major scale.
Although they have their own pattern of whole and half steps, for now we will
simply relate them to their relative major key signature.

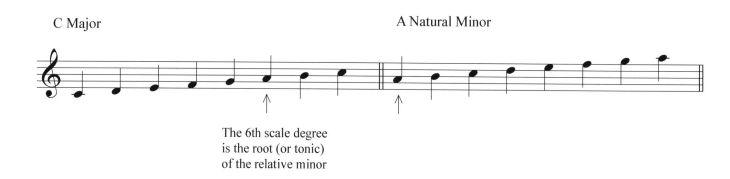

The 6th scale degree is the root (or tonic) of the relative minor

Harmonic & Melodic Minor Scales

There are three minor scales that you will encounter at this level.
For reading purposes, this book focuses on melodic minor scales.

Natural Minor: Uses only the notes from the key signature.
Harmonic Minor: Raises the 7th scale degree.
Melodic Minor: Raises the 6th and 7th scale degree while ascending
and returns to the natural minor 6th and 7th when descending.

A Natural Minor

A Harmonic Minor

A Melodic Minor

© Bradford Werner 2017, Victoria, BC, Canada
Free & Premium Sheet Music & Tab: wernerguitareditions.com
Lessons, Pro Video, & Blog: thisisclassicalguitar.com

Chords & Chord Progressions

Only a partial explaination of chords and chord progressions is neccessary at this time. For now, try to remember the basic difference between major and minor chords and the order of major and minor chords in the harmonized major scale.

Scale Degrees in C Major

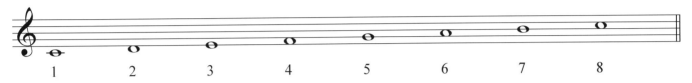

C Major Triad (Three Note Chord) C Minor Triad

Triads and chords can occur in many *voicings* as long as the 1, 3, and 5 of the scale are present.

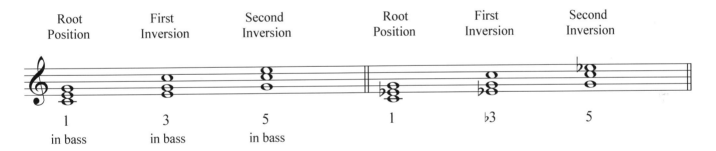

Harmonized C major scale
Chords can be built on each note of the major scale to create chord progressions.
You will be playing many common chord progressions throughout this book.
Capital Roman numerals represent major chords and lower case represent minor chords.
Do not confuse Roman numberal analysis with position marks that are above the staff and followed by a period.

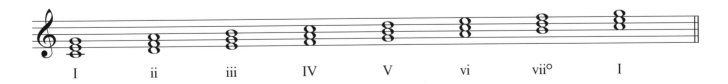

© Bradford Werner 2017, Victoria, BC, Canada
Free & Premium Sheet Music & Tab: wernerguitareditions.com
Lessons, Pro Video, & Blog: thisisclassicalguitar.com

Barre Technique

This technique benefits from watching the YouTube lesson (see preface).

A *barre* (or *capo*) is a technique where more than one string is played by the same left hand finger. Barres almost exclusively use the 1st finger of the left hand. Very little barring occurs in preliminary to grade one repertoire and therefore, not much is used in this book. Students will undergo a further study of barring in my Volume 3 method.

There are many ways to notate barre chords. All three symbols below indicate a barre at the first fret over 3 strings. The Roman numberal indicates the fret number. The number indicates how many of the top strings are barred.

BI3 or CI3 or ₵I

Tips to avoid buzzing and fatigue:
1. Only apply pressure to the exact strings being used (not the entire finger).

2. Let the weight of the left arm pull the barre finger down into the strings, rather than applying too much pressure between the finger and thumb (as a vice).

3. Place your finger close to the fret on <u>all of the barred strings</u>. This is extremely important. The #1 cause of difficulty is the finger being played at an angle where some fretted strings are not close to the fret. Really cozy up close to it!

Barre Examples
We will only be using half barres in this book. Half barres use only the top three strings.
Use your 1st finger of the left hand and place it across the indicated strings.

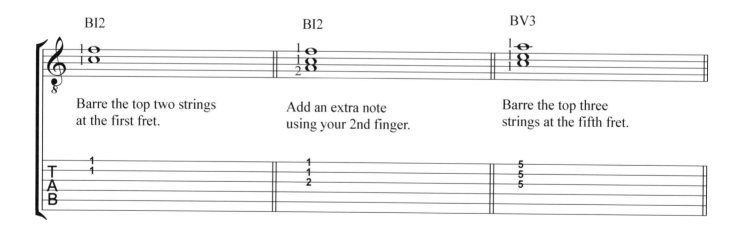

© Bradford Werner 2017, Victoria, BC, Canada
Free & Premium Sheet Music & Tab: wernerguitareditions.com
Lessons, Pro Video, & Blog: thisisclassicalguitar.com

Introduction to Slurs

Slurs are played by plucking the first note and letting the left hand sound the second note.
This technique greatly benefits from watching the YouTube lesson (see preface).
You can find a slur exercise in the technique section (Part 4).

Ascending Slurs (Hammer-ons):
Pluck the first note and 'hammer' the second note down with a left hand finger.
Do not push hard with the slur finger, but instead, move quickly and 'snap' the finger into the string.
Play with an even and slow tempo, but make your movements fast and reflex-oriented.

Descending Slurs (Pull-offs):
Pluck the first note and then pull down with the indicated left hand finger.
This will require both fingers to be on the string for a small moment.
Practice pulling the left-hand finger down (toward your feet) into the string below
(think of it as a left-hand rest-stroke). Also practice pulling down but bypassing the string below.

Slurs are notated similar to phrase marks and ties but the context is usually easy to comprehend.

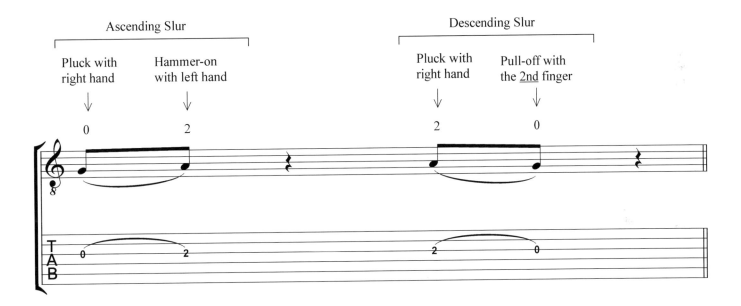

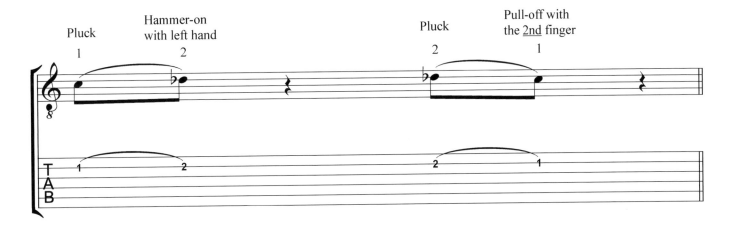

© Bradford Werner 2017, Victoria, BC, Canada
Free & Premium Sheet Music & Tab: wernerguitareditions.com
Lessons, Pro Video, & Blog: thisisclassicalguitar.com

Position Playing

Position playing refers to the location of the left hand on the fingerboard.
Part 1 of this book has some playing in 2nd position.
Part 2 of this book is dedicated to playing in the 3rd and 5th position.
This technique greatly benefits from watching the YouTube lesson (see preface).

The position is named from the location of the 1st finger of the left hand.
If your 1st finger is at the 1st fret you are in 1st position (I.).
If your 1st finger is at the 3rd fret you are in 3rd position (III.).

The position will not always be clear as guitar playing occasionally requires using more
than one finger on the same fret. However, this is a general rule to guide our technique
and to organize our playing.

Position playing is best understood when using a <u>one-finger-per-fret</u> rule.
Remember to keep your thumb behind your 2nd finger at all times regardless
of playing position.

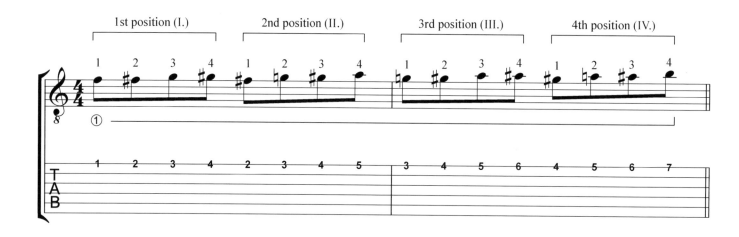

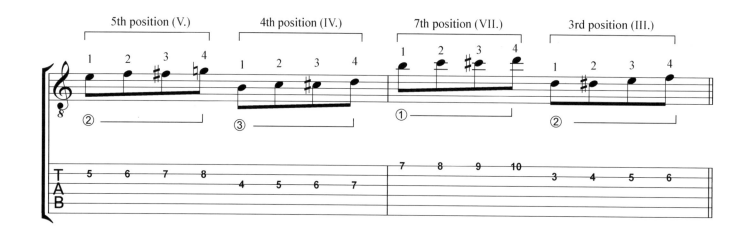

© Bradford Werner 2017, Victoria, BC, Canada
Free & Premium Sheet Music & Tab: wernerguitareditions.com
Lessons, Pro Video, & Blog: thisisclassicalguitar.com

C Major

Practice the scales with multiple right hand fingerings as suggested in parentheses.
The use of the 4th finger on upper strings is discussed in the preface.

One Octave C Major Scale

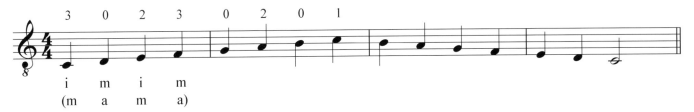

C Major Position Scale

One Octave C Major Arpeggio   C Major Triads (use p, i, m)

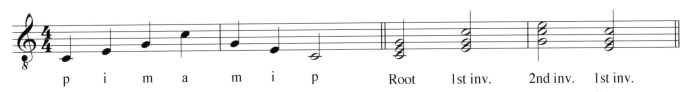

Chord Progression in C Major (strum with p)
The fingering for the G chord will often be required during repertoire.

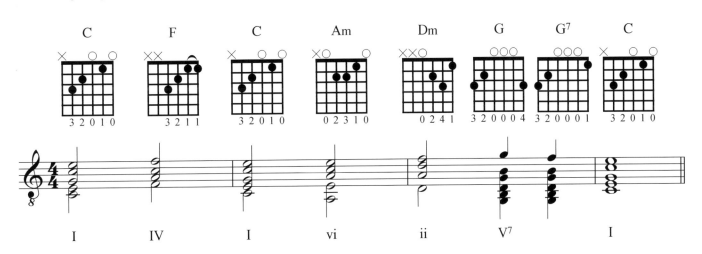

© Bradford Werner 2017, Victoria, BC, Canada

Menuet en Rondeau

Jean-Philippe Rameau (1683-1764)
Originally for keyboard

The student plays the top part.
Play with or without slurs based on your teacher's recommendation.

Allegro
No. 8, Op. 333

Ferdinando Carulli (1770-1841)

This piece alternates between triplets (marked with a 3) and eighth notes.
Triplets are three notes per beat while eighth notes are two notes per beat.
I recommend you use a metronome set to the quarter note to keep an even pulse.

Notice how the upper and lower voice noteheads are often combined for rhythmic and written clarity.

The indicated chords are useful for recognizing basic shapes but you are not expected to know each one.
Chords with slash marks: the first letter indicates the chord, the second letter indicates the bass note.
The notes in chords can appear in many different orders as you learned in the triad exercise.

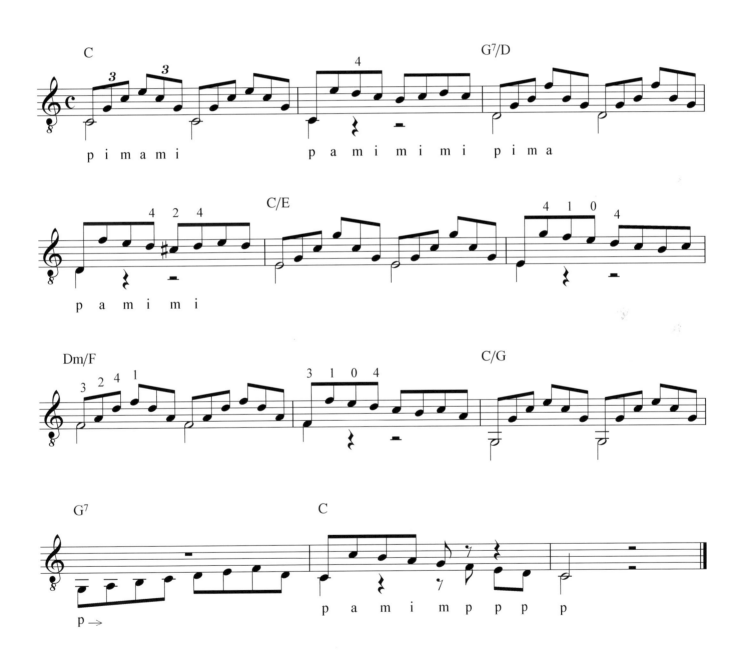

Morning Has Broken

Hymn on a Scottish Tune

There are many great recordings of this song but my favourite is by Cat Stevens.

Play this song in three ways with your teacher or a friend:
1. Play the melody. 2. Strum the chords with p. 3. Invent a fingerstyle accompaniment.

© Bradford Werner 2017, Victoria, BC, Canada
Free & Premium Sheet Music & Tab: wernerguitareditions.com
Lessons, Pro Video, & Blog: thisisclassicalguitar.com

A Melodic Minor

Watch carefully for the brief switch to 2nd position during the position scale.
Due to the position change, play the scale with a one-finger-per-fret rule.

One Octave A Melodic Minor Scale

A Melodic Minor Position Scale

Two Octave A Minor Arpeggio   A Minor Triads (use p, i, m)

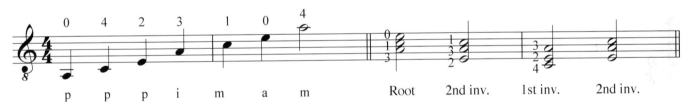

Chord Progression in A Minor (Strum with p)

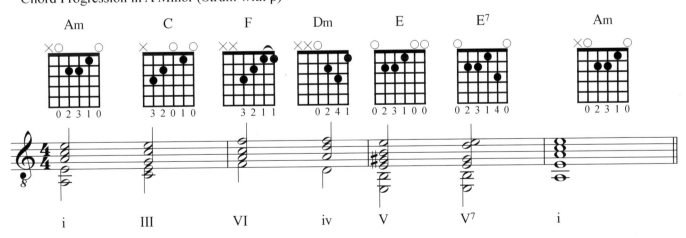

© **Bradford Werner 2017, Victoria, BC, Canada**
Free & Premium Sheet Music & Tab: wernerguitareditions.com
Lessons, Pro Video, & Blog: thisisclassicalguitar.com

Romance No. 14, Op. 168

Joseph Küffner (1776-1856)
Edited/modified for this book

The student plays the top part.

Prelude in A Minor
from Méthode Complète pour Guitare, Op.59

Matteo Carcassi
(1770-1841)

Sustain all notes within each chord and play the bass voice legato.

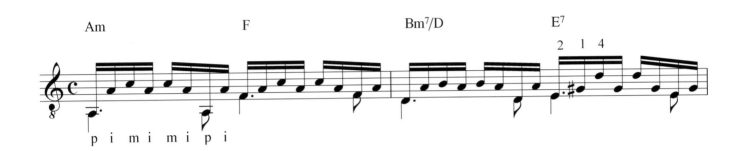

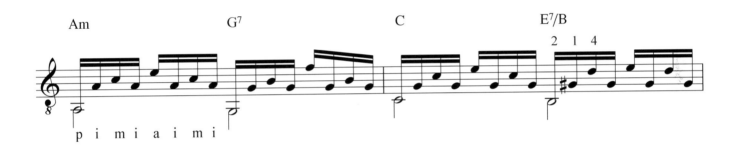

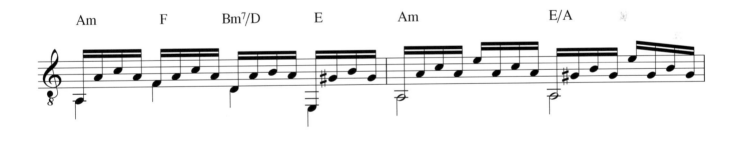

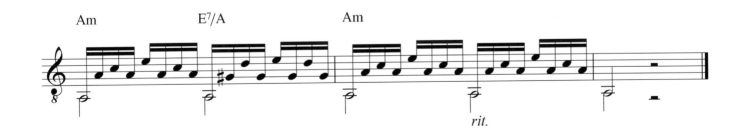

G Major

Two Octave G Major Scale

G Major Position Scale

Two Octave G Major Arpeggio   G Major Triads (use p, i, m)

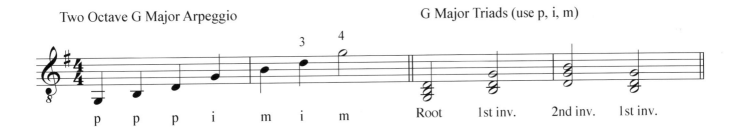

Chord Progression in G Major (Strum with p)

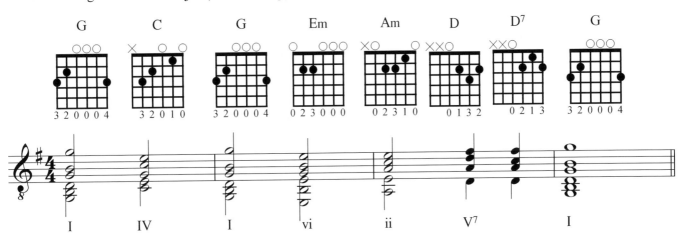

Andante, Op.27

Ferdinando Carulli (1770-1841)
Edited/modified for this book

The student plays the top part.
Guitar two has been written in Carulli's original simplified notation.

Simple Gifts
(Arranging Lesson)

Shaker Hymn
Elder Joseph Brackett
(1797-1882)

This piece demonstrates how to make a very basic solo arrangement.
Notice how the bass notes match the roots of the chords and the upper voice is the melody.

Play in three ways: 1. Melody on its own (upper voice); 2. Strum the chords;
3. Play the full notated arrangement using alternaing i,m for the melody and p for the bass.

© **Bradford Werner 2017, Victoria, BC, Canada**
Free & Premium Sheet Music & Tab: wernerguitareditions.com
Lessons, Pro Video, & Blog: thisisclassicalguitar.com

E Melodic Minor

Due to the accidentals, play this scale with a <u>one-finger-per-fret</u> rule.

Two Octave E Melodic Minor Scale

E Melodic Minor Position Scale

Two Octave E Minor Arpeggio   E Minor Triads

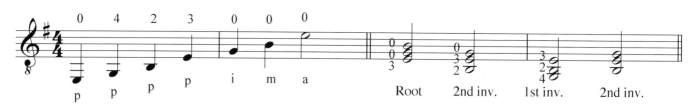

Chord Progression in E Minor (Strum)

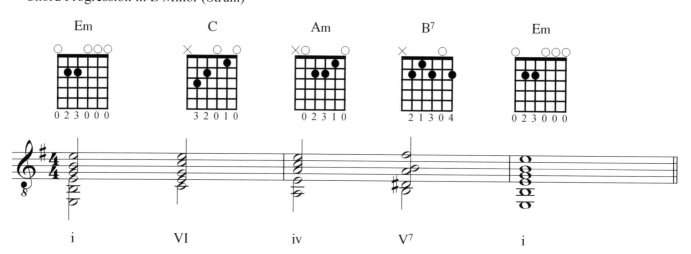

© **Bradford Werner 2017**, Victoria, BC, Canada
Free & Premium Sheet Music & Tab: wernerguitareditions.com
Lessons, Pro Video, & Blog: thisisclassicalguitar.com

Erster Verlust No. 16, Op. 68
(First Loss / Heartbreak)

Robert Schumann (1810-1856)
Originally for keyboard

The student plays the top part.

Prelude in E Minor

Matteo Carcassi (1770-1841)
Edited/modified for this book

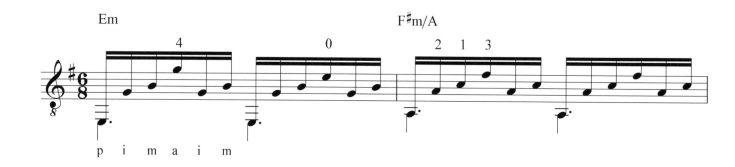
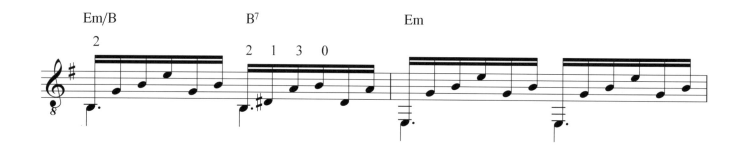
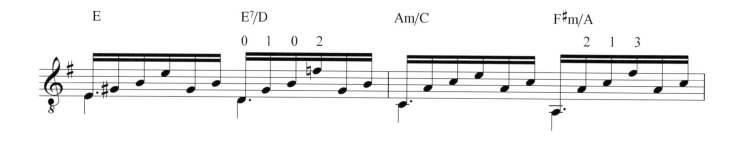
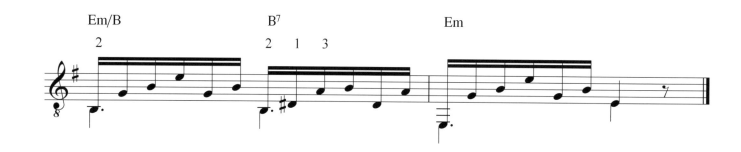

D Major

D Major can be played in either 1st or 2nd position. However, since there are no notes on the 1st fret, I recommend playing all the scale examples in 2nd position to prepare you for position playing in repertoire.

One Octave D Major Scale

D Major Position Scale

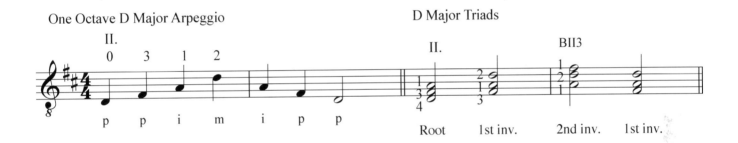

Chord Progression in D Major (Strum)

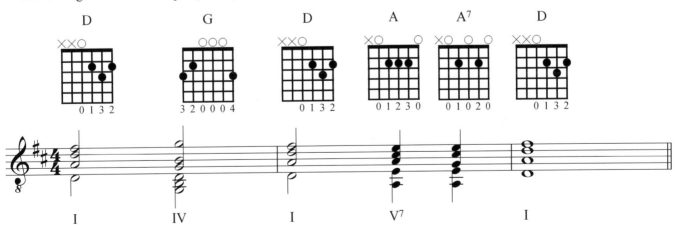

© Bradford Werner 2017, Victoria, BC, Canada
Free & Premium Sheet Music & Tab: wernerguitareditions.com
Lessons, Pro Video, & Blog: thisisclassicalguitar.com

Le Petit Rien

Francois Couperin (1668-1733)
Originally for keyboard

The student plays the top part with i, m. Because compositions often step outside the key with accidentals, more than one position of the guitar will be needed. Watch carefully for changes between 1st and 2nd position.

Allegretto

Rujero

Gaspar Sanz (1640-1710)
Edited/modified for this book

Watch carefully for changes between 1st and 2nd position.
Isolate the first two bars from the last line for extra practice.

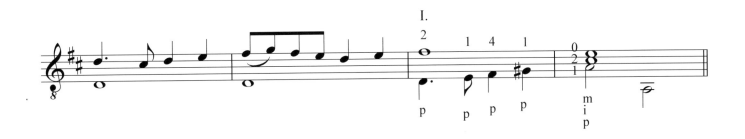

© **Bradford Werner** 2017, Victoria, BC, Canada
Free & Premium Sheet Music & Tab: wernerguitareditions.com
Lessons, Pro Video, & Blog: thisisclassicalguitar.com

A Major

Due to the position change, play this scale with a <u>one-finger-per-fret</u> rule.

Two Octave A Major Scale

A Major Position Scale

Two Octave A Major Arpeggio   A Major Triads

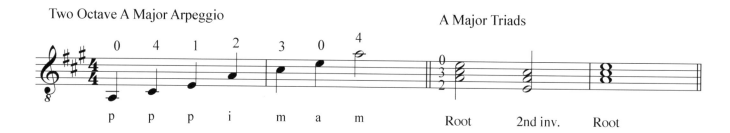

Chord Progression in A Major (Strum)

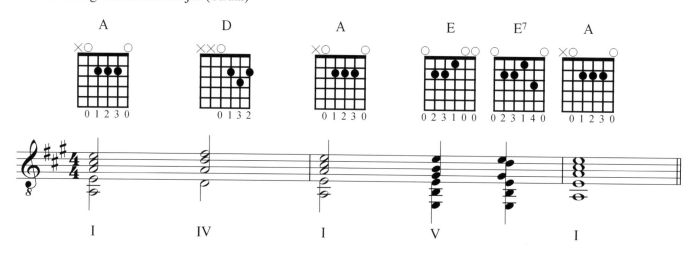

Menuet in A, HWV545

George Frideric Handel
(1685-1759)

The student plays the top part. Notice the special fingering required
to play legato on notes sharing the same fret of adjacent strings.

Prelude in A, No. 4, Op. 114

Ferdinando Carulli (1770-1841)
Edited/modified for this book

The main chords in this arpeggio prelude are A, E7, and D.
The bass note A is often used under the chord forming a *pedal tone*.

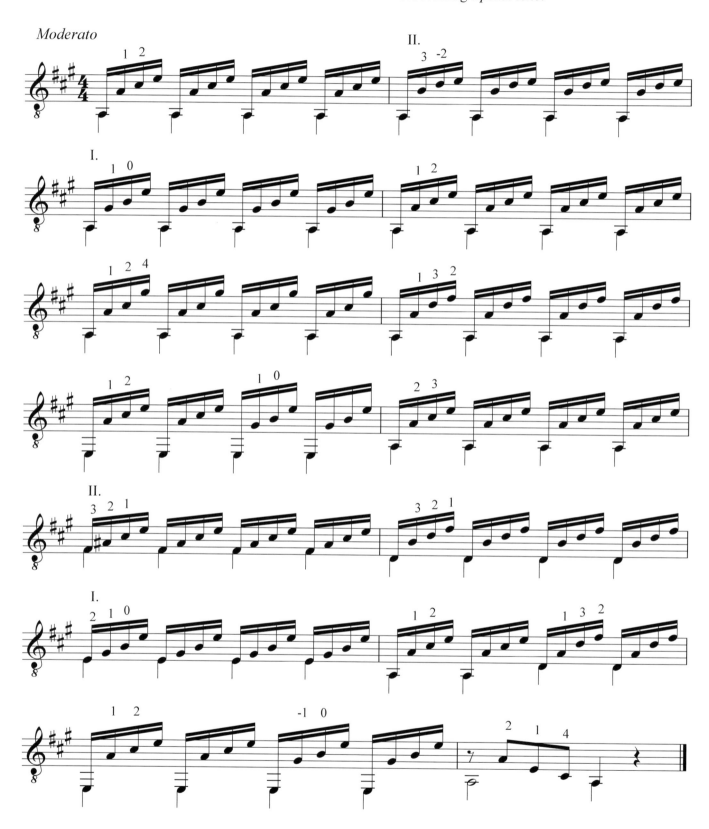

Bound for South Australia

Sea Shanty

My favourite recording of this song is by a band named The Pogues.

1. Play the melody.
2. Strum the chords with two strums per bar.

E Major

Two Octave E Major Scale

E Major Position Scale

Two Octave E Major Arpeggio   E Major Triads

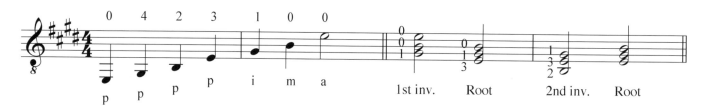

Chord Progression in E Major (Strum)

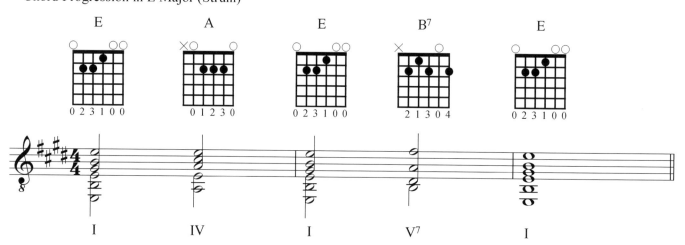

Gavotte

Arcangelo Corelli (1653-1713)
Originally for keyboard

The student plays the <u>bottom part</u>.

Allegretto

Study No. 15, Op. 60

Fernando Sor (1778-1839)

Although the E major scale is played in 1st position, it is often
neccesary to play in 2nd position and alter fingerings to make chord shapes
comfortable for the left hand. Watch the position changes carefully.
Notice how the first two lines follow the same chord progression.
Teachers may wish to assess the diffculty level of this work before assigning it.

F Major

Two Octave F Major Scale

F Major Position Scale

One Octave F Major Arpeggio   F Major Triads

Chord Progression in F Major (Strum)

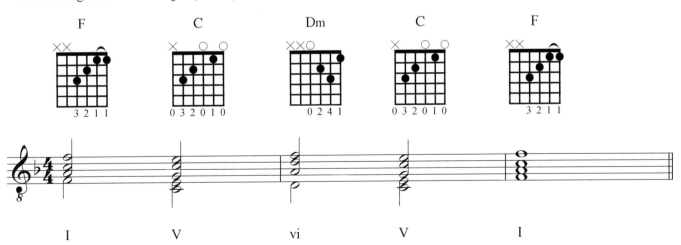

Prelude
The student plays the top part.

Johann Gottfried Walther (1684–1748)
Originally for keyboard

Tempo di Marcia
From Schule für die Guitarre

Johann Kaspar Mertz (1806–1856)

Aim for legato eighth notes and stately chords. There are a few places where you have jump left hand fingers across strings so listen carefully to hear the musical result and sustain notes long enough to avoid a choppy performance.

D Melodic Minor

Due to the Bb on the 3rd string, play this scale with a <u>one-finger-per-fret</u> rule.

One Octave D Minor Scale

D Minor Position Scale

One Octave D Minor Arpeggio   D Minor Triads

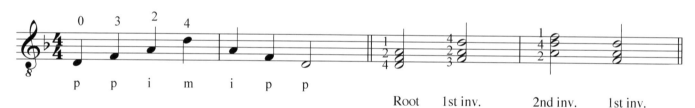

Chord Progression in D Minor (Strum)

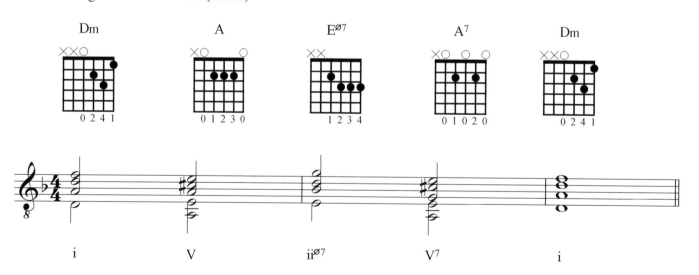

Riguadon

Jean-Philippe Rameau (1683–1764)
Originally for keyboard

The student plays the <u>bottom part.</u>

Folies d'Espagne

Anonymous
Edited/modified for this book

The Folía theme is an old European melody that has been arranged countless times from the Renaissance to modern times. This is an edited excerpt from an anonymous Baroque guitar edition. Let notes sustain within the bar regardless of notation.

© Bradford Werner 2017, Victoria, BC, Canada
Free & Premium Sheet Music & Tab: wernerguitareditions.com
Lessons, Pro Video, & Blog: thisisclassicalguitar.com

Bb Major

Due to the notes on the 3rd and 4th frets, play this scale with a <u>one-finger-per-fret</u> rule.

One Octave Bb Major Scale

Bb Major Position Scale

One Octave Bb Major Arpeggio   Bb Major Triads

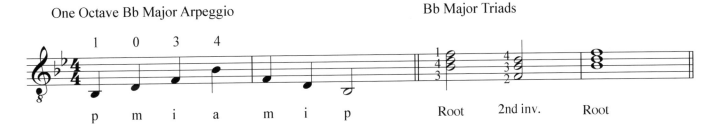

Root   2nd inv.   Root

Bourrée

Georg Philipp Telemann (1681-1767)
Originally for keyboard

The student plays the bottom part.

© Bradford Werner 2017, Victoria, BC, Canada
Free & Premium Sheet Music & Tab: wernerguitareditions.com
Lessons, Pro Video, & Blog: thisisclassicalguitar.com

Reading Music in Upper Positions
Single String Chromatic Scales

These scales teach the musical alphabet up a single string to the 12th fret octave.
Memorize the pattern and say the note names out loud as you play.
The fingering is the same for all the strings/scales.

1st String - E Chromatic

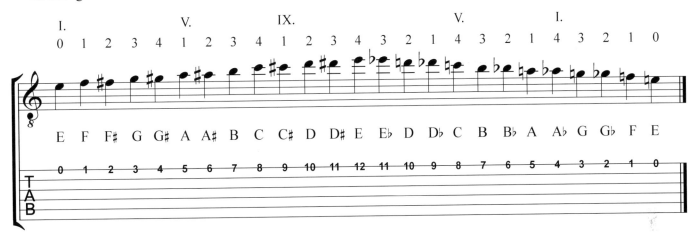

2nd String - B Chromatic

3rd String - G Chromatic

© Bradford Werner 2017, Victoria, BC, Canada
Free & Premium Sheet Music & Tab: wernerguitareditions.com
Lessons, Pro Video, & Blog: thisisclassicalguitar.com

Introduction to 3rd and 5th Position with TAB

This page uses TAB to clarify the location of notes.
These notes will be <u>repeated without tab</u> on the following pages.

When playing in position it is common to use a one-finger-per-fret fingering concept.
Therefore, we will use the 3rd finger for D and G in 1st position for this section.

Notice how the first examples below all contain the same notes but are played in different locations of the fretboard. I recommend you say the note names out loud as you play.

Imitation in 1st, 3rd, and 5th Position

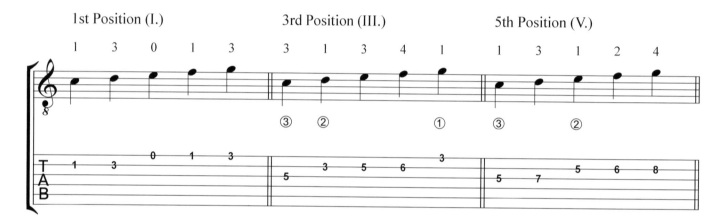

C Major up to the highest note in position
Change positions as indicted by the Roman numberals.

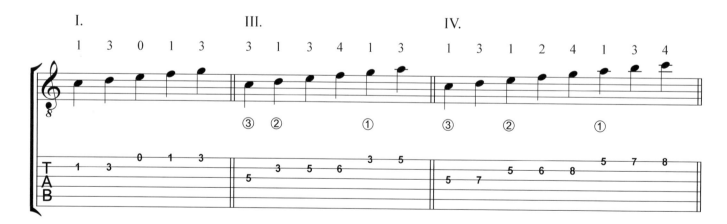

Introduction to 3rd & 5th Position

Although you've already learned these notes with TAB,
it is important to gain experience reading notation.

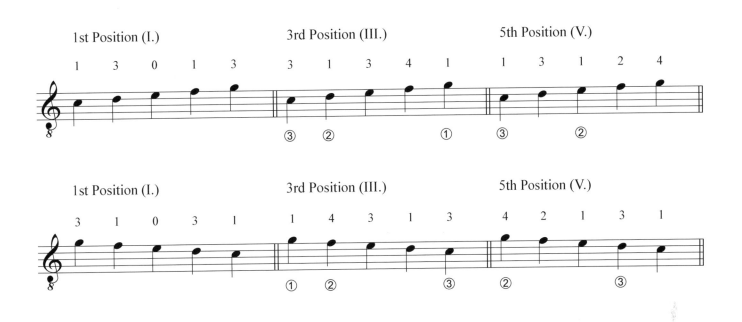

Ode to Joy
Play in 1st postion and then repeat in 3rd and 5th position.

Exercise #1
Play in 1st position and then repeat in both 3rd and 5th position.

Exercise #2 - C Major

Play in 1st, 3rd, and 5th position.

Exercise #3 - G Major

Play in 1st and 5th position.

Exercise #4 - D Major

Play in 5th position.

Exercise #5 - C Major

Play in 1st, 3rd, and 5th position.

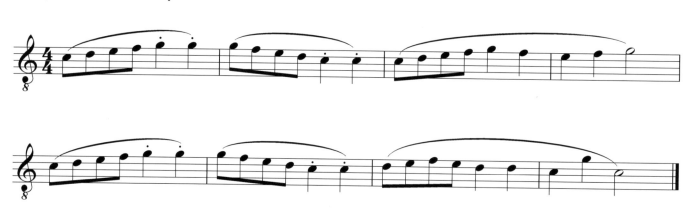

To the Highest Note in Position

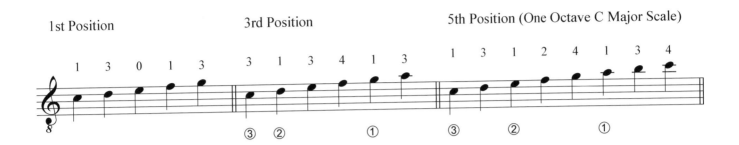

Twinkle Twinkle Little Star
Play in 3rd and 5th position

Exercise #6 - C Major
Play in 5th position

Exercise #7 - E Minor
Play in 5th position

Exercise #8 - F Major
Play in 3rd position

Exercise #9 - A Minor
Play in 3rd position with open bass strings.

Exercise #10 - C Major
Play in 5th position

Joy to the World

Carol
(Antioch/Handel/Mason)

The student plays the melody in 5th position.
The teacher accompanies with chords.

El Noi de la Mare

Traditional Catalan Song

The student plays the top part in 5th position.
This duet is loosely based on Miguel Llobet's (1878–1938) popular solo arrangement.

© Bradford Werner 2017, Victoria, BC, Canada
Free & Premium Sheet Music & Tab: wernerguitareditions.com
Lessons, Pro Video, & Blog: thisisclassicalguitar.com

Estudio

Francisco Tárrega (1852–1909)
Edited/modified for this book

This is an easy arrangement of a solo guitar composition.
Play the entire piece in 5th position. Notice the special fingering
required from bar 3 to bar 4 in order to play legato from one string to the next.

Andantino

Position Shifts

It is often easier to make a legato position change during an open string.
However, there are times when shifting up the same string can also be desirable.

Pay close attention to the Roman numberals, string numbers, and fingering.
Aim for a very legato sound regardless of the type of shift.

Shift on the open 1st string

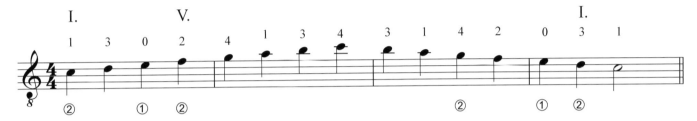

Shift on the 2nd string

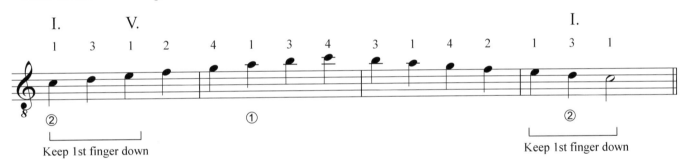

Shift on the 1st string

© Bradford Werner 2017, Victoria, BC, Canada
Free & Premium Sheet Music & Tab: wernerguitareditions.com
Lessons, Pro Video, & Blog: thisisclassicalguitar.com

The Canaries or the Hay
from John Playford's Musick Hand-Maid (1678)

Anonymous

This piece will be played in the 1st and 5th position.
The shift uses the 4th finger as a guide along the 2nd string from the note before.
Remember to sustain notes for as long as possible. Notice the special fingering
at the end of the third line in order to play legato across the strings.

© Bradford Werner 2017, Victoria, BC, Canada
Free & Premium Sheet Music & Tab: wernerguitareditions.com
Lessons, Pro Video, & Blog: thisisclassicalguitar.com

Feng Yang Flower Drum

Chinese Folk Song

Notice the special fingering required in bar 2, 3, and 8
in order to play legato from one string to the next.

For the purposes of this book this piece will be played in the 1st and 5th positions.
The shifts occur after the ends of phrases to avoid disrupting the musical flow.
Sustain the final note of the phrase long enough that the shifts are not noticable.

Captain O'Kane

Turlough O'Carolan
(1670-1738)

The student plays the melody, the teacher accompanies with chords.
This piece will be played in the 1st and 5th positions.
The shifts occur on the open 1st string.

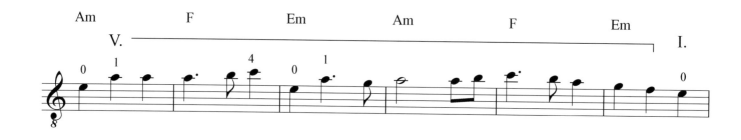

© Bradford Werner 2017, Victoria, BC, Canada
Free & Premium Sheet Music & Tab: wernerguitareditions.com
Lessons, Pro Video, & Blog: thisisclassicalguitar.com

Tips for Counting Rhythms

1. Experience should precede knowledge. The student should learn rhythm primarily through listening, feel, and imitation. After getting 'a feel' for the music, then theory and structure should follow. Work on rhythm with the teacher and/or watch the video lessons.

2. Always be <u>able</u> to sing and play the rhythm feeling only the beat of the time signature (<u>without subdividing</u>).

3. When practicing a difficult rhythm, count various subdivisions of the beat (as shown below).

Example 1

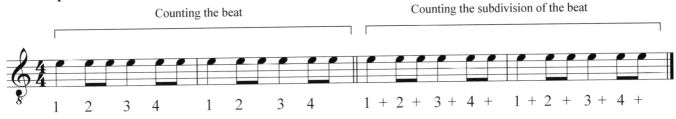

Example 2a - Three identical examples with different counting
The lower voice in this example shows the division of the beat (do not play/sing it).

Counting the beat

Subdividing to the eighth note

Subdividing to the sixteenth note

Example 2b
These are identical to Example 2a but without the subdivisions shown in the lower voice.

Counting the beat

Subdividing to the eighth note

Subdividing to the sixteenth note

Subdividing where needed

Example 3 - Triplets

Counting the beat

Subdividing the triplet where needed

© Bradford Werner 2017, Victoria, BC, Canada
Free & Premium Sheet Music & Tab: wernerguitareditions.com
Lessons, Pro Video, & Blog: thisisclassicalguitar.com

Familiar Rhythmic Groupings

Rhythms that students find difficult are often just divisions of simpler rhythms.
By comparing similar rhythms (without time signatures or tempo markings),
we can discover which rhythms can be understood to be similar.

Stop after each example (double barline). <u>Play the notes in each group at the same relative tempo.</u>
For instance, play the eighth notes in bar 2 at the same tempo as the quarter notes in bar 1.
All the examples in each group should sound exactly the same. This will help the student
understand how rhythms *function* in similar ways.

Four Evenly Spaced Notes

Long, Short, Short

Short, Short, Long

© Bradford Werner 2017, Victoria, BC, Canada
Free & Premium Sheet Music & Tab: wernerguitareditions.com
Lessons, Pro Video, & Blog: thisisclassicalguitar.com

Dotted Rhythms

Short, Long, Short

Three Evenly Spaced Notes

Open String Rhythm Exercises

Work through these exercises with your teacher and/or watch the YouTube lesson videos.
Play treble strings with *i, m* and bass strings with *p*

4/4 Time Signature
Four quarter notes in each bar
Also called *Common Time*

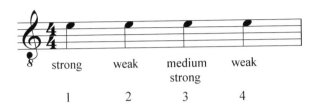

No.1 - Quarter, Half, & Whole Notes

No.2 - Common Time

No.3

3/4 Time Signature
Three quarter notes in each bar

No.4 - Dotted Half Note

No.5

No.6

No.7 - Quarter & Half Note Rests
Remember to stop the sound on the rests by placing the next right hand finger on the string.

No.8 - Whole Note Rest

No.9

No.10 - Dotted Half Note Rest

No.11

No.12

No.13 - Eighth Notes

No.14 - Eighth notes often get beamed in groups (starting from strong beats).

No.15 - Eighth notes beamed to the quarter note.
This example is identical to the rhythm in No. 14 but with different beaming.

No.16

No.17

No.18

2/4 Time Signature
Two quarter notes in each bar

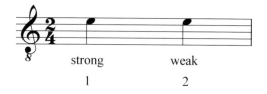

No.19

No.20 - Eighth Notes Rests
Remember to stop the sound on the rests by placing the next right hand finger on the string.

No.21

No.22

No. 23 - Ties, sustain for both note values (do not repluck the 2nd note).
Notice how the first two bars are identical sounding despite the different notation.

No.24

No.25

No.26 - Dotted Quarter Notes

No.27

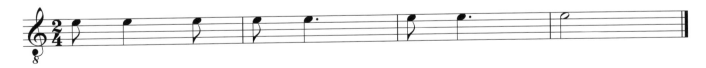

No.28

No.29

No. 30

2/2 Time Signature
Two half notes in each bar. Also called *Cut Time*.
Although Cut Time has four quarter notes in each bar it is not the same as Common Time.
When Cut Time is written, it is specifically telling you that the emphasis is on the half note pulse.
Remember, the half note is now the primary beat so quarter notes only count for half a beat.

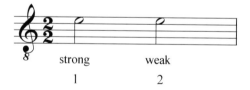

No.31 - Cut Time

No.32

No.33

6/4 Time Signature
Six quarter notes in each bar.
Feel two main beats per bar based on the dotted half note, the notes are in groups of three (1-2-3 and then 4-5-6). This is referred to as compound duple time with the main emphasis on beat 1 and 4. This is often counted and conducted with only two beats per bar showing the emphasis on the main beats (as shown in parentheses).

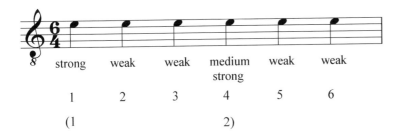

No.34 - Count 6 beats per bar and then repeat feeling only the 2 strong beats per bar.

No.35

3/8 Time Signature

Three eighth notes in each bar.
Depending on the tempo, the feel is often one strong beat for each bar, especially in faster tempos.
Up to this point only quarter and half notes have represented the beat; remember, the eighth note is now the primary beat.

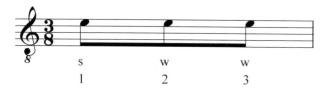

No.36

No.37

No.38

6/8 Time Signature

Six eighth notes in each bar.
Feel two main beats per bar based on the dotted quarter note.
This is referred to as compound duple time with the main emphasis on beat 1 and 4.
This is often counted and conducted with only two beats per bar showing the emphasis on the main beats (as shown in parentheses).

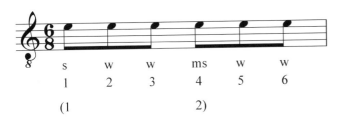

No. 39 - Count 6 beats per bar and then repeat feeling only the 2 strong beats per bar.

No.40

No.41

9/8 Time Signature

Nine eighth notes in each bar.
Feel three main beats per bar based on the dotted quarter note.
This is referred to as compound triple time with the main emphasis on beat 1, 4, and 7.
This is often counted and conducted with only three beats per bar showing the emphasis on the main beats.

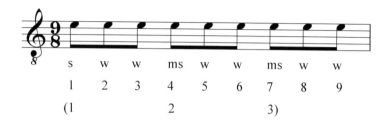

No. 42 - Count 9 beats per bar and then repeat feeling only the 3 strong beats per bar.

No. 43

No. 44

No.45 - Triplets - Notice how this example sounds the same as No.44 despite the different time signature.

No.46

No.47

No.48

No.49 - Triplets Next to Eighth Notes

No.50 - Sixteenth Notes

No.51

No.52 - Sixteenth Note Rests

No.53

No.54

© **Bradford Werner 2017, Victoria, BC, Canada**
Free & Premium Sheet Music & Tab: wernerguitareditions.com
Lessons, Pro Video, & Blog: thisisclassicalguitar.com

No.55 - Dotted Eighth Notes
Notice that this is just a smaller division of the dotted quarter note but the feel is the same.
For example, "Deck the Halls" could be sung to either rhythm depending on the time signature.

No.56

No.57

No.58

No.59

No.60

Right Hand Exercises

Right-hand alternation on open-strings
I recommend using a metronome and marking your speed goals to track your progress.

Tips

- ✓ Practice with staccato and legato articulation.
- ✓ Practice with both rest-stroke and free-stroke.
- ✓ Accent the first note of each eighth or sixteenth note group.
- ✓ Try free-stroke with a rest stroke on the first note of each group.

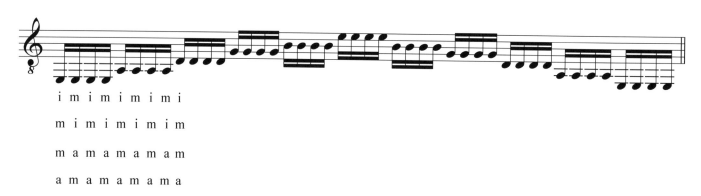

© Bradford Werner 2017, Victoria, BC, Canada
Free & Premium Sheet Music & Tab: wernerguitareditions.com
Lessons, Pro Video, & Blog: thisisclassicalguitar.com

Two-Voice Right Hand Patterns

Use free-stroke when first practicing this page. Once completed you can try playing with a light rest-stroke in the thumb and free-stroke with the fingers.

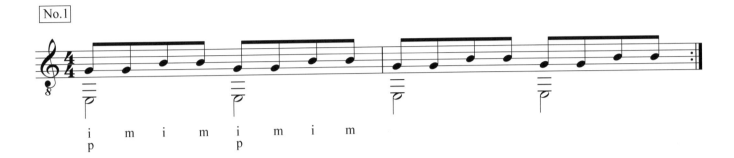

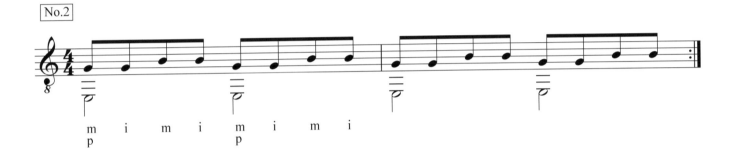

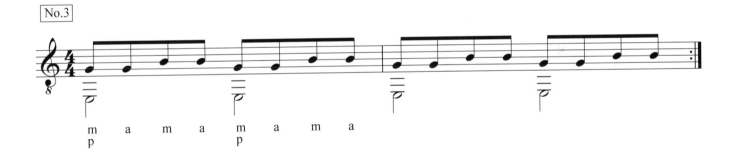

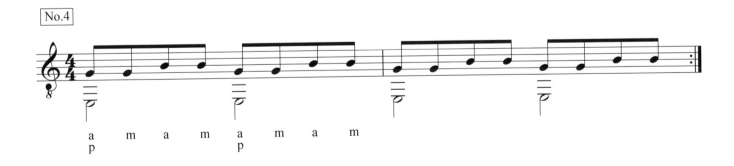

© Bradford Werner 2017, Victoria, BC, Canada
Free & Premium Sheet Music & Tab: wernerguitareditions.com
Lessons, Pro Video, & Blog: thisisclassicalguitar.com

Awkward String Crossings

Use free-stroke when first practicing this page. Once completed you can try playing with a light rest-stroke in the thumb and free-stroke with the fingers.

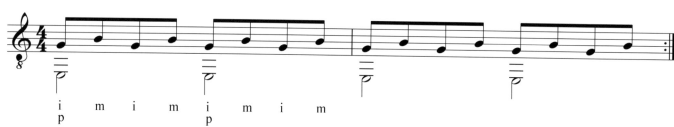

No.2
Reaching i over m is considered an awkward string crossing but it is an essential skill.

No.3

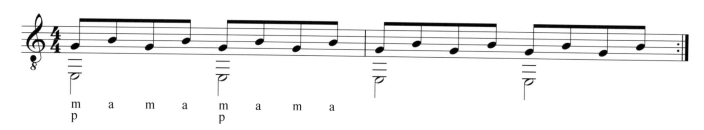

No.4
Reaching m over a is also an awkward string crossing.

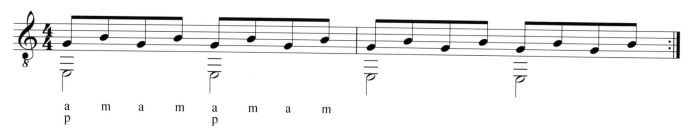

© Bradford Werner 2017, Victoria, BC, Canada
Free & Premium Sheet Music & Tab: wernerguitareditions.com
Lessons, Pro Video, & Blog: thisisclassicalguitar.com

Basic Arpeggio Patterns with p, i, m, a

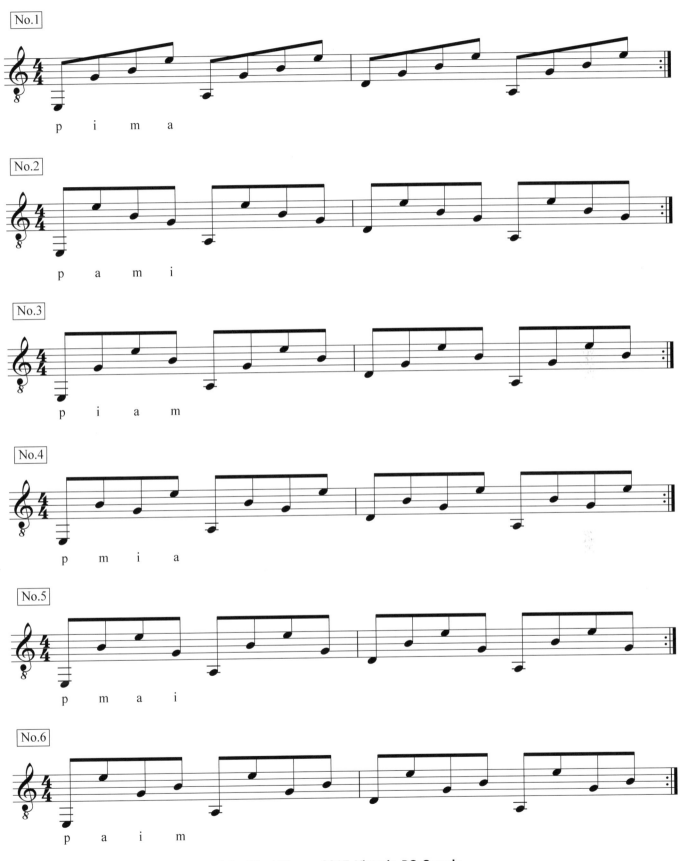

Arpeggio Patterns in Two Voices

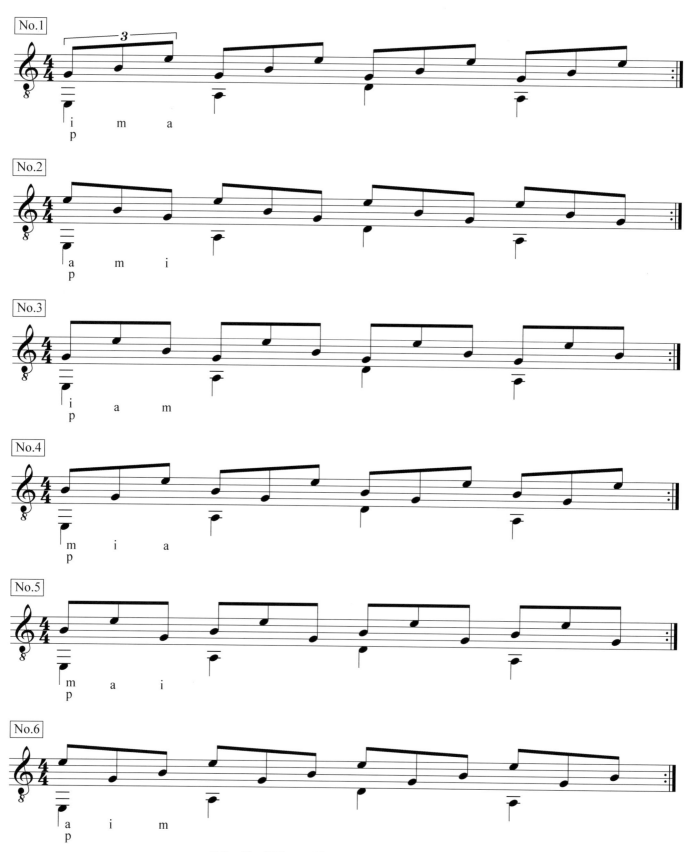

Selected Giuliani Exercises from Op. 1

Students may omit the E on the 4th string from the final chord or
sweep the thumb over two strings as written.

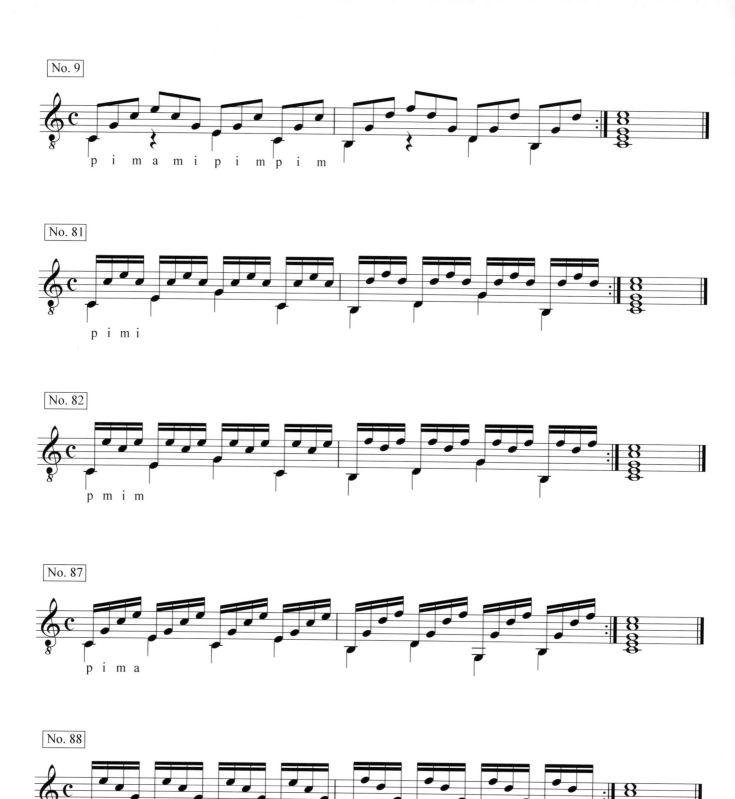

Speed & Stability Exercise

The staccato articulation can be accomplished by placing the next available right hand finger on the note thereby stopping its sound. This will train the right hand fingers to be prepared for the next note well in advanced, making it an excellent speed and stability exercise. Also practice with alternating m-i / m-a / a-m

Left Hand & Synchronization Exercises

1-2-3-4 on all strings
Use your thumb for the three bass strings and i,m for the top three strings.
Descend using the same pattern.

1 and 4 on all strings
Keep the left hand aligned with the strings.
Descend using the same pattern.

© Bradford Werner 2017, Victoria, BC, Canada
Free & Premium Sheet Music & Tab: wernerguitareditions.com
Lessons, Pro Video, & Blog: thisisclassicalguitar.com

Finger Independence

Place the indicated fingers on the notes marked with an x and hold for the entire line.
Do not play the notes with an x, only hold your fingers on the string at the indicated frets.
Play the last two notes of each bar using the indicated finger.

Ascending Slurs (Hammer-Ons)

An introduction to slur technique is given in the preface.
TAB has been added to clarify the fret and position of the exercises.
Use your thumb for the three bass strings and i,m for the top three strings.
Descend using the same pattern.

© Bradford Werner 2017, Victoria, BC, Canada
Free & Premium Sheet Music & Tab: wernerguitareditions.com
Lessons, Pro Video, & Blog: thisisclassicalguitar.com

Descending Slurs (Pull-Offs)

Use your thumb for the three bass strings and i,m for the top three strings.
Descend using the same pattern.

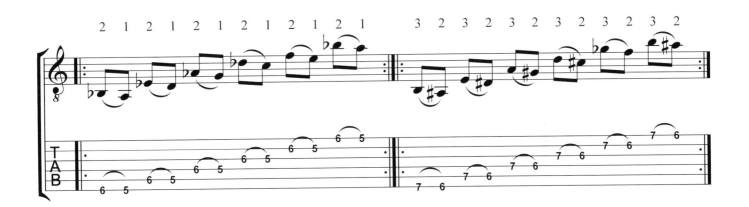

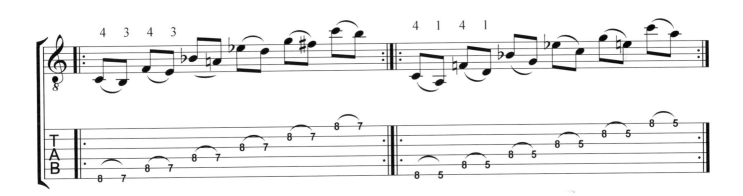

© Bradford Werner 2017, Victoria, BC, Canada
Free & Premium Sheet Music & Tab: wernerguitareditions.com
Lessons, Pro Video, & Blog: thisisclassicalguitar.com

Two Moveable Major Scale Patterns

Moveable patterns can be played anywhere on the guitar and in multiple keys, all you have to do is repeat the same finger pattern from a different root (starting note/fret). Clarify with your teacher and watch the video lesson. Use alternating i-m / m-i / m-a / a-m

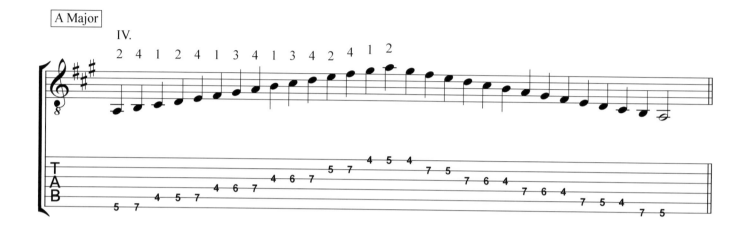

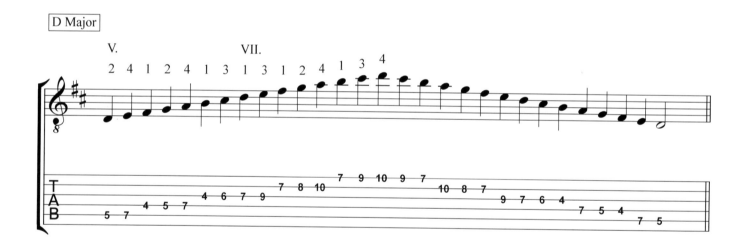

© Bradford Werner 2017, Victoria, BC, Canada
Free & Premium Sheet Music & Tab: wernerguitareditions.com
Lessons, Pro Video, & Blog: thisisclassicalguitar.com

Chromatic Scales

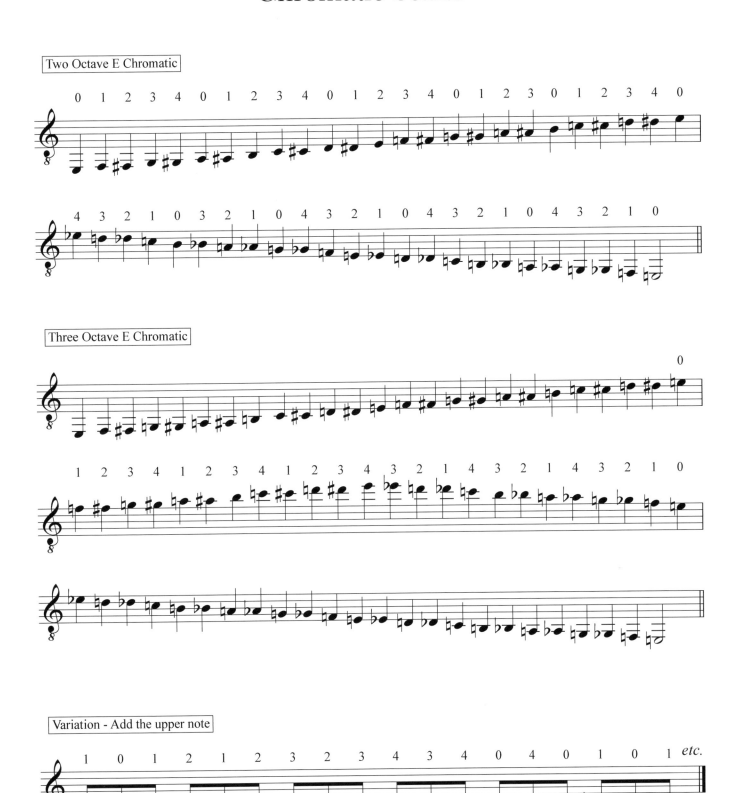

Made in the USA
Columbia, SC
22 October 2018